TRUE CRIME

COPS AND ROBBERS

John Townsend

www.raintreepublishers.co.uk

Visit our website to find out more information about **Raintree** books.

To order:

☎ Phone 44 (0) 1865 888113

▤ Send a fax to 44 (0) 1865 314091

💻 Visit the Raintree Bookshop at **www.raintreepublishers.co.uk** to browse our catalogue and order online.

First published in Great Britain by
Raintree, Halley Court, Jordan Hill, Oxford OX2 8EJ,
part of Harcourt Education.
Raintree is a registered trademark of Harcourt
Education Ltd.

Editorial: Melanie Copland and Sarah Chappelow
Design: Lucy Owen and Kamae Design
Picture Research: Hannah Taylor and
Ginny Stroud-Lewis
Production: Carmilla Smith

Originated by RMW
Printed and bound in China
by South China Printing Company

ISBN 1 844 438139
11 10 09 08 07 06
10 9 8 7 6 5 4 3 2 1

British Library Cataloguing in Publication Data
Townsend, John
Cops and Robbers – (True Crime)
364.1'552
A full catalogue record for this book is available from
the British Library.

Acknowledgements
Alamy Images pp. **title** (David Crausby), **4** (Paul
Bourdice), **12** (Brand X Pictures), **14–15** (Comstock
Images), **23** (Adrian Chinery), **27** (Gabe Palmer), **28**
(Tim Graham), **28–29** (David Crausby), **32** (Joe
Sohm), **39** (Travelstock44), **42–43** (Shout), **43**
(Photofusion Picture Library/Ray Roberts); Associated
Press pp. **14** (Joe Don Buckner), **19**, **40** (New
Associated Press); Corbis pp. **8** (Sygma/Pierre
Vauthey), **11** (Bettmann), **16** (Burstein Collection),
16–17 Sygma/Yves Forestier), **20** (Charles & Josette
Lenars), **26** (Douglas Kirkland), **26–27** (Reuters),
30–31 (Lucidio Studio Inc), **33** (Bettmann), **38** (Sergio
Dorantes), **41** (Patricia Santos/Reuters); Daily News
Pix pp. **18–19**; Getty Images pp. **5**, **6** (Photodisc), **15**
(AFP), **22**, **24** bottom (Hulton Archive), **24** top
(Hulton Archive); **25** (Hulton Archive); Mary Evans
Picture Library pp. **6–7** (Bruce Castle Museum); PA
Photos pp. **21** left, **21** right (Fiiona Hanson); Rex
Features pp. **13**, **22** (Rex Features); The Art Archive p.
17 (Nasjonal Galleriet Oslo / Album/Joseph Martin
Munch Museum/ Munch-Ellingsen Group, BONO,
Oslo, DACS, London 2005); The Kobal Collection pp.
4–5 (Warner Bros), **5** (Morgan Creek/Vah Redin), **5**
(20th Century Fox), **7** (Bryna Prods/United Artists),
8–9 (Morgan Creek/Vah Redin), **10** (20th Century
Fox), **10–11** (20th Century Fox), **18** (Warner
Bros/Dirck Halstead), **32** (Warner Bros), **34** (20th
Century Fox TV/Stf Prod./ Stl Prod./Fox
Productions/Craig Blankenhorn), **35** (Universal
TV/Wolf Film), **36**, **37** (Warner Bros), **36–37**
(Spelling/Goldberg); Topham Picturepoint p. **33**.

Cover photograph of a police car and suspect
reproduced with permission of Corbis/Peter Turnley.

Every effort has been made to contact copyright
holders of any material reproduced in this book.
Any omissions will be rectified in subsequent
printings if notice is given to the publishers.

The paper used to print this book comes from
sustainable resources.

Contents

Daylight robbery 4

Robberies long ago......................6

Robbing records 12

Big-time raids 18

Cops...................................24

In the news 30

On screen..............................34

Strange but true.......................38

Find out more..........................44

Glossary 46

Index..................................48

Any words appearing in the text in bold, **like this**, are explained in the Glossary. You can also look out for them in the Word Bank at the bottom of each page.

Daylight robbery

Ever since the first caveman hit his neighbour with a rock and stole his dinner, robbers have been at work. So have people who try to stop them. Cops and robbers have tried to get the better of each other for hundreds of years.

Every day, robbers grab things that belong to others. Every day, police grab robbers and lock them up! Stories of cops and robbers are found in books, television, and films. They are in newspapers, too. There must be thousands of robbers out there. But do not worry, there are millions of police officers in the world.

Not many people know this...

According to recent figures for reported crime, the country where you are more likely to be robbed is Spain. It has almost half a million robberies every year. More than 12 out of every 1000 people are likely to get robbed each year. There is help at hand, though. Spain has over 115,000 cops to hunt down the robbers.

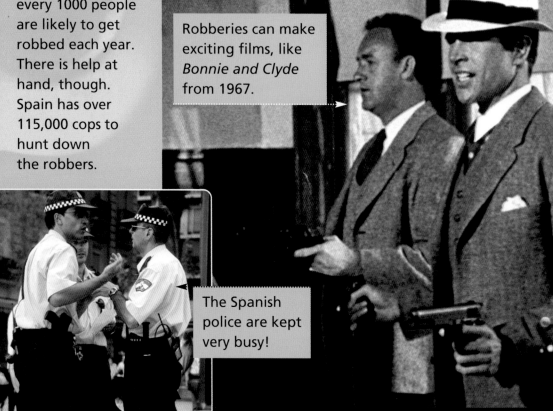

Robberies can make exciting films, like *Bonnie and Clyde* from 1967.

The Spanish police are kept very busy!

Word Bank   mugging robbing in the street with threats or violence

Thieves with threats

Although gangs of bank robbers hit the news headlines, most robbers work alone. They usually strike in dark streets and their crimes last less than a minute. They often use a weapon to carry out a **mugging**. Robbers are thieves who use threats or violence to get what they want. Sometimes they get more than they want – a tough prison sentence!

There are many types of thief about, including:
- pickpockets in the street
- shoplifters
- burglars who break into houses.

Find out later...

Who were the robbers of long ago?

What was the biggest robbery on record?

What was the biggest robbery that never was?

Robberies long ago

Ancient robbers

Thousands of years ago, the rich leaders of ancient Egypt were buried with their treasure inside pyramids. These were often guarded. Pyramids were built with a maze of passages so that robbers would get lost inside. People also warned that a curse would strike anyone who broke in. Even so, robbers would sometimes rob the tombs of gold.

Some people think crime today is far worse than it used to be. But robbery has always been a problem. In fact, crime was often much worse than it is today. People just did not get to hear about robberies the way they do today.

A crime wave hit London in 1728. As there was no police force then, people paid "watchmen" to protect them in the streets at night.

Watchmen will keep watch on 40 houses each. They will be armed with firearms and swords. Each will have a bugle to sound an alarm in time of danger. Lamps will be set up in the street to help stop robberies.

Word Bank

civil war   war between people of one country
gangster   member of a gang of criminals

Crime waves

There were robbers of all kinds in the 1700s.
Highwaymen robbed people on the roads.
Pirates robbed people at sea. In the United States
in 1790, a law made anyone who would "aid or
advise robbery on land or sea" a criminal.

It was not until the 1860s that robbers caused
big trouble in the United States. After the
American **Civil War**, a lot of men who had been
soldiers travelled west to start new lives. Some of
them joined gangs and robbed banks. They also
robbed **stagecoaches**. Another crime wave hit US
cities 50 years later. **Gangsters** with machine guns
robbed banks and sped off in cars.

Vikings were
violent robbers.

Viking robbers

Perhaps the most
feared robbers in
history were the
Vikings. From
750 to 1050 A.D.,
these people from
Norway, Sweden,
and Denmark sailed
in longships to rob
many countries.
They attacked
villages and stole
gold from their
churches. They also
kidnapped people
to use as slaves.
Vikings were
thought of
as pirates and
their raids were
often violent.

Highwaymen leapt out shouting
"Your money or your life!"

highwayman   person who robs travellers on a highway
stagecoach   wagon pulled by horses, carrying mail or passengers

Robbing banks

Wherever money is kept, robbers will want to get their hands on it. Since the first banks were built, robbers have found ways to snatch the cash. The United States's first bank robbery was said to be in 1798. Over US$162,000 was stolen from the Bank of Pennsylvania in Philadelphia. The thief broke in at night using copied keys.

In New York, USA, the first bank robbery was similar. In 1831 Edward Smith stole US$245,000 from City Bank. He, too, used a set of copied keys. The theft was discovered the next day.

Hold-ups!

In the 1800s, all you needed to be a bank robber was a gun and a fast horse. Today, banks are far better protected. Bulletproof screens, alarms, and cameras cut down a robber's chance of success. Most bank crime today involves stolen credit cards.

Criminals today do not need to break into vaults to steal money.

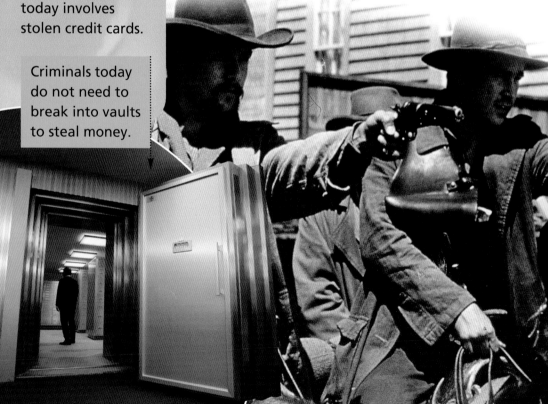

The Great Bank Robbery

The greatest bank robbery in the history of the United States was in 1876. It was in Northampton, Massachusetts. One night, seven men broke into the house of one of the staff from Northampton National Bank. They tied up the whole family and got the keys to the bank's **vault**. They stole over US$1 million. That would be worth over US$26 million today. In time, the robbers were caught.

The person who lost the most in the Northampton bank robbery was Judge Forbes. US$200,000 of his money was stolen. That would be US$3.3 million today! At the time, he was asleep in the second floor flat of the same building as the bank!

Facts and figures

The table below shows the number of robberies on each day of a sample week in the United States in 2000.

Monday	1423
Tuesday	1354
Wednesday	1293
Thursday	1236
Friday	1634
Saturday	473
Sunday	88

The most popular time for banks to be robbed is between 9 a.m. and 11 a.m. on Fridays. Robbers expect the banks to have more money at the end of the week.

Robberies happened a lot in the Wild West.

vault locked room for keeping valuables in at a bank

Trains were a target for robbers.

Banks on wheels

Robbers knew that trains often carried gold or money between towns along the "railroad". Trains sometimes carried rich passengers, too. Gangs would lie in wait and climb on board a train when it slowed down to climb up a hill. In the United States, 1870 to 1890 was a busy time for train robbers. After that, faster trains and armed guards helped to stop train robberies.

Trains

Robbing a train could be a quick way to get rich. One of the first train robberies was in 1866 in Indiana, USA. Masked robbers demanded keys to the safes that were kept on board the train. The passengers were terrified as the robbers emptied a safe and threw another from the train. The five Reno brothers carried out the robbery. They galloped away with US$10,000. They tried more train robberies, but before long they had all been killed. Violent robbers are not known for their long and happy lives!

This train robbery went wrong in the 1969 film *Butch Cassidy and the Sundance Kid*. They blew up the money they were trying to steal!

The last train robbery of the Wild West

In 1923, the 23-year-old D'Autremont twins and their teenage brother robbed a train in Siskiyou, California. They hid in a tunnel and climbed on the train as it slowly climbed up a hill. They used dynamite to blast open the end of the train. This killed a man and set fire to the train. The robbers could not see what they were doing because of the smoke. They got angry and shot some of the passengers before running away. They were not very successful robbers.

A few years later they were all in prison serving **life sentences**.

The Great Train Robbery

The biggest train robbery in the UK was near London in 1963. A gang of robbers held up a train, attacked the driver, and stole bags full of cash worth £2.6 million. The police soon caught all the robbers. The amount stolen would be worth over £40 million today.

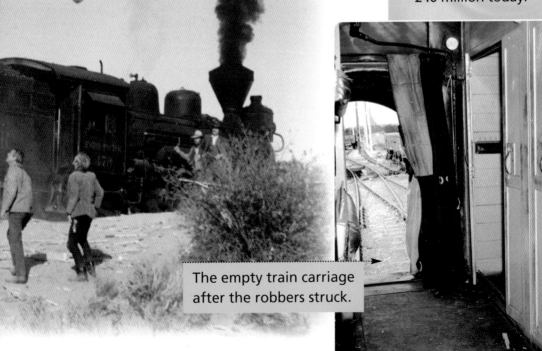

The empty train carriage after the robbers struck.

life sentence being sent to prison for the rest of a person's life

Robbing records

Some robberies end up in the record books. This is usually because of what has been stolen.

Diamonds are forever

Eighty per cent of the world's diamonds are traded through Antwerp's Diamond Centre, Belgium. It has been the centre of the world's diamond industry since the 1600s. Millions pass through the city every year. They are worth a fortune. Robbers are always lurking!

Largest jewel robbery

According to *Guinness World Records*, the biggest jewel robbery so far was in 2003. It took place at the Antwerp Diamond Centre in Belgium. Thieves emptied **vaults** in a weekend raid, but it is a mystery how they broke in. The theft was not discovered until the following day. About £65 million worth of diamonds had simply disappeared.

> " These guys are brilliant with keys and alarm systems. They don't need to use violence. "
>
> (Joris Van der Aa, journalist from Antwerp)

Largest mugging

A messenger was taking a briefcase full of **bonds** across London, UK in 1990. At 9.38 a.m. on 2 May, a **mugger** jumped out with a knife and snatched the briefcase. He ran off – straight into the record books. The value of the bonds was £292 million. That is the largest amount ever snatched on the street. The only thing is, the robber could never change the bonds into real money. Within hours, all the banks knew about the robbery and would not deal with the bonds. The police later traced all but 2 of the 301 bonds.

Cops find robber

Police believe that Patrick Thomas, a robber from London, UK, carried out the "largest mugging" in 1990. He was found dead from a gunshot wound in 1991 before he could be charged with the robbery.

Could thieves target the Antwerp Diamond Centre again?

Would you believe it?

In the United States in 2004, the world's oldest robber was sentenced. He was 92-year-old Red Rountree (below). He got a 12-year prison sentence for robbing a bank in Abilene, Texas. During the previous 5 years he had robbed 3 banks. Each time he handed a note to cashiers that said: "This is a robbery. Do as I say or you get hurt."

Big money

In 1950, an armed gang robbed a security company called Brinks in Boston, USA. They got away with over US$2.5 million in cash and cheques. At the time, it was the largest robbery in US history. Seven robbers did the job in dark coats, gloves, and Halloween masks. They got through locked doors using copies of keys and reached the staff who were counting money. Brinks offered a reward of US$100,000 for help in catching the robbers. It took 6 years before all the robbers were caught and sent to prison. The police found much of the stolen money. This crime did not pay off after all.

Word Bank

chaos great confusion, when lots of things are happening
sapphire blue precious stone

Smash and grab

In 1976, a gang of armed robbers took over the British Bank during the **civil war** in Beirut, Lebanon. The thieves cleared out all the deposit boxes. These boxes were small safes where people left their valuables for safe keeping. But these deposit boxes were not safe for long. No one really knows how much the gang stole, but all the money, jewels, and gold bars may have been worth £22 million. It took 2 days to rob the bank and load up their trucks. In all the **chaos** of the civil war, no one took any notice of the robbers.

Unwelcome wedding present

Dasha Strelkova was a wealthy Russian woman living in London in 2003. She was soon to marry a British man. Just before the wedding, thieves stole a **sapphire** worth over half a million pounds from her safe. The sapphire was not **insured**. Not a good start to the wedding!

Sometimes even safe deposit boxes are not safe from thieves!

insure promise by a company to pay money to someone if their property is damaged or stolen

15

Art robbers

Art robbery is big business. It is the fourth largest crime after drug dealing, money theft, and illegal weapons trading. About £150 million worth of lost and stolen art has been **recovered** around the world in the last 10 years.

In an art gallery in England in 1997, a man asked to see a painting by **Picasso**. When he was shown the painting, he pulled out a shotgun. He grabbed the painting worth over half a million pounds and fled in a taxi. He might have got away with the robbery if he had not left the painting's frame in the taxi. It was covered with his fingerprints!

Storm on the Sea of Galilee by Rembrandt.

Word Bank
abandon leave something behind
Picasso famous 20th-century painter

Van Gogh was a Dutch painter who lived from 1853 to 1890. After his death, his paintings became very valuable.

In 1991, two robbers stole twenty very famous Van Gogh paintings. They snatched them from the Van Gogh Museum in Amsterdam, Holland. It was one of the shortest art robberies on record. The robbers **abandoned** the paintings less than an hour later, outside a nearby railway station. All of the paintings were recovered, including the **priceless** *The Potato Eaters*. Who knows why the robbers left such valuable paintings behind and ran off?

Edvard Munch's painting *The Scream*.

Art robbers steal *Scream*

On 22 August 2004 gunmen stole Edvard Munch's famous painting *The Scream* in a daring raid on a museum in Norway. Armed men burst into the building and took the **priceless** work off the wall in front of terrified visitors. They escaped in a waiting car. Another of Munch's *Scream* paintings was stolen 10 years earlier. Police got it back.

Van Gogh's famous painting *The Potato Eaters*.

priceless too valuable to have a price
recovered get something back again after it has been stolen

Big-time raids

Some record-breaking robberies have been done by robbers taking even bigger risks. They planned every detail of their daring raids, often known as **heists**. They did not always succeed.

1978

The record for the largest ever heist in the United States was smashed in 1978. A gang stole US$6 million worth of money and jewels from New York's JFK Airport. It was from the warehouse of Lufthansa Airlines. The robbers had help from a man working inside the airport. He told them how to get into the warehouse and how many guards would be working that day.

"Don't mess with us!"

Robbers on film

A few films have featured the true story of the 1978 robbery at New York's JFK Airport:
- *Goodfellas*
- *The Big Heist*
- *The Ten Million Dollar Getaway*.

Police investigating a van thought to have been used in the Lufthansa Airline heist.

Word Bank   heist robbery that is carefully planned and organized

Success and failure

The robbers used a van and guns. Two men stayed behind as lookouts while the other four jumped from the van. They tied up airport staff and then switched off the airport alarms before getting to the safes. They backed the van into the warehouse, loaded up, and sped off. Despite the guns, not a single person was killed.

This was a "gangland" robbery involving many criminals caught up in **organized crime**. No one could be trusted and before long, most of the robbers had "gone missing" or been killed by each other. The police caught some of the robbers, but the money was never found.

The mastermind

The man who planned the robbery of the Lufthansa Airline warehouse was James Burke (below). Everyone called him Jimmy the Gent. He had been a criminal for a long time. The police caught up with him and he died in prison in 1996.

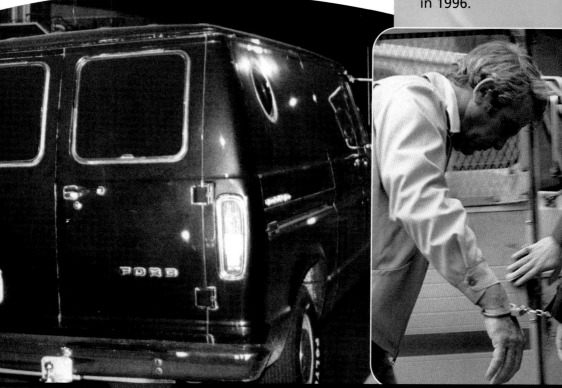

Stolen gold

One of the biggest robberies in the UK was a surprise, even to the robbers. They had no idea how much gold they would find.

A company called Brinks Mat had a warehouse at Heathrow Airport in London, UK. When a guard turned up for work in November 1983, the alarm was turned off to let him in. That was when the gang of robbers struck. They ran in wearing masks and carrying guns. They tied up all the guards, but could not get into the main safe. So they poured petrol over a guard. They said they would set fire to him unless he told them how to open the safe. They got what they wanted.

Fact file

Brinks Mat robbery

When: 26 November 1983
Where: Brinks Mat warehouse, Heathrow Airport, London, UK
Who: Six armed robbers
What: £26 million in gold bars
Outcome: Some of the robbers sent to prison. 3 tonnes of gold still missing.

All this gold was a nice surprise for the Brinks Mat robbers.

Inside help

Two hours later, the gang had filled their van with tonnes of gold, and were gone. The police spoke to all the guards. One of them looked a bit worried. The police discovered his sister lived with a well-known criminal. Now they knew who they were after. Before long they had tracked down some of the gang. Two of the robbers went to prison for 25 years each. Others were caught later, but the rest of the gang has not been found.

A man called Kenneth Noye was a suspect. He was arrested after he stabbed a policeman who was keeping watch on him. In court Noye was proved to have links with the Brinks Mat robbers. He was found guilty of having some of the stolen gold. He went to prison in 1985.

Best behind bars

Kenneth Noye served 9 years in prison for dealing with the stolen gold. Two years after his release in 1996, he lost his temper with a car driver and killed him. Noye is now serving a **life sentence** for murder.

The police used this evidence in their investigation into the Brinks Mat robbery.

The Millennium
Star diamond.

Millennium robbery

As the UK's capital city, London needed something special to mark the year 2000. The Millennium Dome by the River Thames was the answer. It was full of displays for visitors to see. One of the displays included the Millennium Star. This is a very rare egg-sized diamond, worth over £200 million. A gang of robbers wanted it. Wearing gas masks, they drove a bulldozer through the Millennium Dome's fence. The gang attacked with sledgehammers, nail guns, and gas bombs. A speedboat was waiting to race them and the diamond away. But things did not work out as planned. The police were ready and waiting!

What they said:

"This would have been the largest robbery in the world."
John Shatford, Metropolitan Police.

"They are not like ordinary south London robbers."
John O'Connell, Police **Flying Squad**.

"I was 12 inches from payday. It would have been a blinding Christmas!"
Bob Adams, robber.

Thieves crashed into the Millennium Dome.

Word Bank

attempted robbery trying to commit robbery, but caught in the act

Big risk

Leading up to the Millennium robbery, the police knew that a gang was planning to strike – but when? They had to be ready day after day. The diamond was secretly replaced with a **fake**. The public carried on visiting. They did not know that police were nearby dressed as cleaners, with guns hidden in their clothes.

At 9.30 a.m. on 7 November 2000, the bulldozer burst in. Masked robbers jumped out, throwing gas bombs. The police shouted "freeze!" and the gang fell to the ground. In all, over 100 police officers took part. Luckily, no one was hurt in the biggest robbery that never was.

The trial

It was 2002 before the five members of the gang went to court. A sixth member had died the year before. Apart from the boat driver, who went to prison for 5 years for "plotting to steal", the other men were found guilty of **attempted robbery**. They went to prison for a total of 66 years between them.

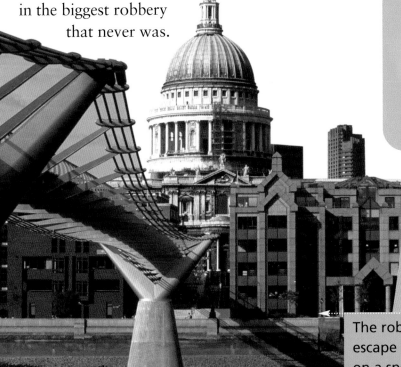

The robbers planned to escape down the Thames on a speed boat.

Cops

Cops and robbers in films, television, and computer games often give us the wrong idea about police life. A lot of police work goes on "behind the scenes". It is not all exciting car chases!

In the beginning

In Roman times, rich landowners paid groups of men to guard their property from robbers. The people who paid the "police" had a lot of power over them. If you paid them, the police had to do as you said.

In the 1700s, the city of London began to pay watchmen to guard the streets at night. In time, a more organized police force developed.

Why are police called "cops"?

Police have been called "cops" for years. Why? Which of these do you think is the most likely reason?
a) The letters "c, o, p" stand for "constable on patrol".
b) The word is short for "copper", because police often wore copper badges.
c) "Cop" was an old word meaning "to catch".
d) Police uniforms once had copper buttons.

Turn to page 44 to find the answer.

The Bow Street Runners were early crime fighters.

Word Bank

census counting of people in a country, city, or town
marshal US government officer similar to a sheriff

Early cops

1750
The Bow Street Runners were formed in London. This was a small group of men who tried to keep criminals off the streets.

1790
In the United States, **marshals** were responsible for recording the population in their districts in the very first **census**. They became important in keeping the law.

1829
The first proper police force started in the UK. Robert Peel began an organized police force in London. Policemen were called "Peelers" or "Bobbies" after him. They wore long, dark blue coats and tall hats, which they could use to stand on to look over walls. Their only weapon was a **truncheon**.

1844
There were around half a million people living in New York City, so officials decided to start up a full-time police force.

First cops in Australia
"It is true that I can set up a police force, but who can make a policeman? ... Where shall I get a gentleman fit to do such a duty who will give up his time for so small a sum?" said Governor Hindmarsh of South Australia in the 1830s. It was 1839 before he found twenty men willing to join his police force.

Australian police in 1937.

truncheon short, thick stick carried by police officers as a weapon

Canine cops

It was not until the 1920s that the police in the UK tried using different breeds of dog to "sniff out" robbers. The most popular was the German shepherd. These dogs are intelligent, with a good sense of smell and hearing. They now play an important role in police work around the world. They track criminals, control crowds, and sniff out drugs, explosives, or human remains.

The use of police dogs in the United States started in the 1970s. Today they are a huge part of police work across the country.

disqualified banned from doing something
suspect someone thought to have committed a crime

K-9 patrol

A four-legged police officer caught four **suspects** in Brisbane, Australia, in 2002. When a policeman pulled over a speeding car, four men jumped out and ran off. Police dog Bodie was let out of the police car to give chase. Bodie raced off and within minutes found the four men hiding in the shadows.

The 21-year-old driver was charged with dangerous driving. He was also a **disqualified** driver and had false number plates on the car. With him off the roads, Brisbane became a little safer. All thanks to police officer Bodie!

The long nose of the law

Police dog Jake caught a 34-year-old man breaking into storage units in Kirkland, Washington, USA. The thief ran off, but Jake was faster. Both were soon rolling on the ground. Jake's handler arrested the man, who had been driving a stolen car with a loaded gun inside. Score: Jake 1, thief 0.

Police dogs are important members of the police force.

LAPD

Los Angeles Police Department (LAPD) in the United States is over 150 years old. It was set up after the murder of one of the city's **marshals** in 1853. "The Los Angeles Rangers" were formed to fight street crime. They were the start of the LAPD. The next 20 years were violent times in the city. It seemed the robbers had the upper hand.

Even by the 1900s, there were still only 70 officers struggling to keep the peace. In 1918, 17 police officers were killed on duty in just 6 months. That year a **Flying Squad** with two "high powered automobiles" and two officers joined the battle to fight crime.

PROTECTING OUR FUTURE...
THE CHILDREN OF LOS ANGELES

A Los Angeles policewoman on the beat.

Word Bank   matron woman who worked in a police station or prison with women prisoners

Female cops

At one time people thought it was shocking that women could be police officers. The nearest things to women police officers were **"matrons"** in California, USA. They looked after female prisoners in the 1890s.

In 1909, Alice Stebbins Wells asked the Mayor of Los Angeles if the city could have a policewoman, who could make arrests. In 1910, Wells became the first policewoman. Two years later there were three policewomen and three police matrons in the LAPD. Soon, other US cities followed, and other countries, too. By 1937, the LAPD had 39 policewomen. Today it has hundreds.

Cop car chases

- Most chases begin when a driver does not pull over when told to by police officers. Most arrests made after a chase are for crimes such as robbery.
- The LAPD makes more than 500,000 traffic stops per year. Chases only happen in a small number of these.
- An LAPD helicopter helps with about 40 per cent of chases.

Los Angeles police have a lot of crime to fight.

In the news

True crime stories appear in newspapers all the time. Cops and robbers make the news nearly every day. Now and again, the robbers get away with it – for a while.

Test drive getaway car

A man test-driving a car in 2004 found that it worked just fine as a getaway car. He had been driving with the car salesman in the passenger seat, when they stopped at a bank in South Ogden, Utah, USA. He ran inside, robbed the bank and drove off without the salesman.

Robber returns cash because of wife

(Goettingen, Germany, March 2004)

A robber who stole a till full of cash returned it an hour later because his wife nagged him. The man took the till from a shop in Goettingen, Germany. He soon came back with the cash (£1300) still in the till. He told the shop assistant his wife had given him such a hard time that he had to return it. The man then drove off in his car. Police started a search, but did not find him.

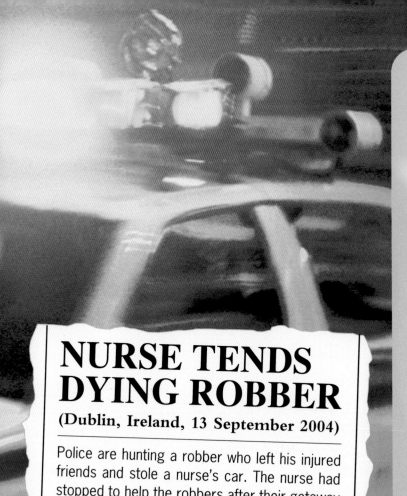

NURSE TENDS DYING ROBBER

(Dublin, Ireland, 13 September 2004)

Police are hunting a robber who left his injured friends and stole a nurse's car. The nurse had stopped to help the robbers after their getaway car crashed. One of the robbers, Michael Brady (24), died. A second man, in his twenties, was seriously hurt in the accident and is under guard in hospital. He has not been named.

The crash happened as the three men fled from a petrol station after robbing it. When the nurse stopped to help, one of the men drove off in her car. Police later found her car **abandoned**.

The gang had driven at high speed from the robbery but lost control of their getaway car.

Robbers caught in getaway car

TIP – if you rob a bank, wait till you get home to count the cash!

An armed man walked into a bank in Bellaire, Texas, USA, in 2005 and demanded cash. He left and jumped into a car driven away by a woman. Police found the couple nearby – counting the money they had just stolen. Both were arrested on the spot.

A close shave!

In Glynn County, Georgia, USA, 34-year-old James Blaze robbed a bank before going to get a haircut. "All of a sudden this young guy just steps in and asks for a haircut," said the barber. "I joked, 'you're not the bank robber I've just heard about on the news are you?' He just smiled and came on in."

Little did the barber know he was talking to the bank robber, who kept very cool and calm. Then the police arrived. They arrested Blaze on the spot. They also **recovered** the bank's money. The only thing the robber got away with was a free haircut!

Did Robin Hood really rob the rich and give to the poor?

Robbin' Hood?

A robber in Romania was arrested in March 2004 when he was found giving away stolen goods. The 30-year-old was arrested in a hostel where he was handing out clothes, jewellery, and money to homeless people. A week earlier the man had stolen goods worth £1000 from a shop.

James Blaze got a free haircut – and his name in the paper!

Bonnie and Clyde

Craig Pritchert and his girlfriend, Nova Guthrie, robbed banks across the western United States from 1997 to 1999. The couple were known as a modern-day "Bonnie and Clyde" after the famous **gangsters** of the 1930s. Pritchert would carry a handgun into banks, tie up the staff and leave with bags of money. Guthrie drove the getaway car. Pritchert was sentenced to twenty-two-and-a-half years in prison. Guthrie was also sent to prison.

"I would like to say sorry to the bank staff for what I put them through," Pritchert said after he was sentenced. Perhaps he should have thought about that before!

The real Bonnie and Clyde.

The big one – failed

In 2004, UK police were ready and waiting for a gang about to rob a warehouse near Heathrow airport in London. The gang of 6 robbers hoped to grab £80 million worth of gold and cash. But over 100 police officers were lying in wait. They arrested the whole gang without a single shot being fired.

On screen

Cop shows

Police dramas, reality shows, and crime phone-ins appear most nights on television. These are some of the most popular crime shows in the United States:
- *LAPD: Life on the Beat*
- *COPS*
- *America's Most Wanted*
- *L.A. Dragnet*
- *Law and Order*

Cops and robbers have always made great entertainment. You only have to look in any shop that sells DVDs to see the number of crime films. Most nights there are "cop shows" on television. We cannot seem to get enough of cops and robbers on screen. Repeats of old series from years ago still appear on television.

Most people know the names of famous American cop shows from the 1970s and 1980s:
- *Cagney and Lacey*
- *Colombo*
- *Starsky and Hutch*

Between them, these characters must have caught a lot of robbers!

John Walsh, the host of the TV show *America's Most Wanted*.

Fighting crime on television

Police programmes have helped to catch many real robbers. *Crimewatch UK* and *America's Most Wanted* get the public to keep a look out for criminals on the run. Many of the criminal cases they show bring big responses. The public help to solve many cases.

Long ago, the police put "wanted posters" around towns. These showed pictures of robbers they wanted to catch. Today, millions of viewers see criminals on television screens, and often recognize them. They might even be living right next door!

LA Dragnet

The original *Dragnet* began in 1949 as a radio drama in the United States. It moved on to television in 1952. It ran through the 1950s and 1960s. Today's *LA Dragnet* features a group of detectives in the LAPD robbery/**homicide** squad. It uses stories based on Los Angeles' rich crime history, as well as today's news headlines.

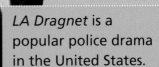

LA Dragnet is a popular police drama in the United States.

homicide killing, or murder, of one person by another

Old films

The first Keystone Kops films were made in 1912 in the United States, before films had sound. Mack Sennett was a maker of silent films and he thought cops and robbers would make good comedy. He put many comic chases in his films about these clumsy cops.

The Keystone Kops.

The big screen

Films about cops and robbers have filled cinemas for over 100 years. Some have simply been called *Cops and Robbers*. The first with that title was made in 1903.

The battle against good and evil usually makes a good story. Then there is the question: will the "baddies" get away with their crime? How will the cops find them, and how will they find the clues?

Some films even have bad cops and good robbers for a change! But the one thing we always expect in a "cop film" is a good chase. Film-makers have to keep finding exciting ways to entertain us.

Small screen to big

Starsky and Hutch was a successful television cop series in the 1970s. It ran for 4 years, with the actors David Soul and Paul Michael Glaser playing the hero cops. In 2004, the *Starsky and Hutch* film came out. Still set in the 1970s, it shows how the cops meet up and tackle their first big case together. They drive around in a red-and-white Ford Torino. Ben Stiller played Dave Starsky and Owen Wilson played Ken Hutchinson.

Once more, cops and robbers brought chases and this time – laughs – to the screen.

Car chases were a big part of *Starsky and Hutch*.

Crime and comedy

Despite crime being a serious business, it can get some laughs, too. These films about cops and robbers mix drama and comedy:
- *Beverly Hills Cop*
- *Police Academy* (shown above)
- *The Italian Job*
- *Rush Hour*

Strange but true

Can you believe it?

In September 2004, three armed guards were delivering cash to a bank in Malaysia when one of them dropped his shotgun. It went off as it struck the floor, shooting five customers. One of the customers said, "I heard the blast and fell, as both my legs were shot." People were rushed to hospital – while the guard had some explaining to do to the police.

With all the books, films, and television series about cops and robbers, you would think the real world could never be as **far-fetched** as all the made-up stories. Think again! Real life is often far stranger than **fiction**.

In 1997, David Posman knocked out the driver of an armoured van and grabbed the bags of money from the back of it. He could only carry four of them, and staggered off down the street in Providence, Rhode Island, USA. Each bag contained US$800. Together they weighed nearly 55 kilograms (120 pounds) as they were all full of pennies. Police soon caught up with him!

Banks in Malaysia need armed guards, but not clumsy ones!

Word Bank   far-fetched hard to believe or imagine

Clumsy crooks

A 1975 bank raid in Rothesay, Scotland, ended up just like a comedy film. On their way in to the bank, three robbers got stuck in the revolving doors. Staff had to help them out. The robbers came back later and told the staff they were robbing the bank. The staff thought they must have been joking and just laughed at the robbers. So one of the robbers tried to jump over the counter. He twisted his ankle and lay on the floor as the others ran off. They got stuck in the doors again!

Shoplifter arrested by 100 cops (2004)

A shoplifter was in the middle of stealing sweets and drinks from a petrol station in Germany. What he did not know was that coaches full of police had pulled up outside on their way to a meeting. They all watched the thief in action. When he came out, 100 cops surrounded him. He was arrested!

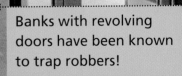

Banks with revolving doors have been known to trap robbers!

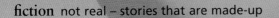

fiction not real – stories that are made-up

Granny robber

In 2004, a judge gave Margaret Thomas-Irving (below), a grandmother from Connecticut, USA, 6 years in prison for bank robbery. He ordered her to pay a fine of US$15,000 and called her "a one-grandma crime wave."

The 58-year-old robbed 2 banks while visiting her son. He was not very happy about it. After all, he was a police officer!

The robber grandma looks shocked at being caught!

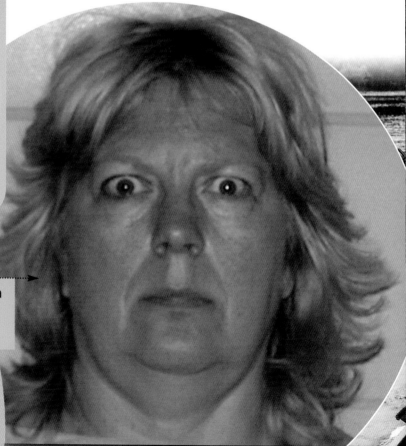

Crazy crimes

A burglar who broke into an art gallery through a skylight window gently lowered himself down on a rope. The trouble was, he then had to call police for help. He could not climb back up again.

CCTV cameras filmed the man in the gallery at East Lansing in Michigan, USA, in July 2004. When he knew he was stuck inside, the thief used the gallery's phone. He called the police. They soon arrived and arrested him. The owner of the gallery watched the video and said, "This guy was a total loser!"

CCTV close-circuit television

Food for thought

Brazil has more than its share of robbers. Some of them seem to take anything. In São Paulo in 2004, a gang of five children robbed an ice cream shop at gunpoint. Aged between eleven and sixteen, they took ice cream, sweets, and drinks from the shop. They ran away, but were caught by police moments later as they were eating the evidence!

Another gang in Rio de Janeiro stole food. They took meat from a butcher's shop, cans of drink, and then stole a car. Police had no idea who they were and said, "All we know is, they like a good barbecue."

Not many people know this...

There are a lot of police officers out there. India has one police officer for every 1000 people. That may not seem very many, but it means there are over 1 million police officers in India alone! That is quite a few more than all the police in the United States and the UK put together.

River police on the lookout for trouble.

41

Robbery victims

It might seem as if we are all at great risk from robbers. In fact, your chance of being a robbery **victim** is very low. Less than 0.8 per cent of the world's people are robbed in a year. In the UK and Australia it is 1.2 per cent, in the United States it is just 0.6 per cent.

And finally...

Even though robberies take place every day, many of them fail. Even those that seem to be well planned often leave clues behind. Many robbers get caught. Prisons are full of failed robbers!

Many studies tell us that most robbers prefer to strike:

- in big cities
- at night – mainly after 8.00 p.m.
- in winter when it is dark earlier
- where there are few **witnesses**
- where there is a quick escape route.

Very few people are **mugged** in daylight when other people are around. So do not have nightmares!

Police can now find more clues than ever at crime scenes.

Word Bank

deter put someone off doing something
forensic scientific investigation to help solve crimes

The fight goes on

The battles and chases between cops and robbers will always amaze us. True crimes will continue to fill newspapers. Robbery stories will always sell books and films.

Although robbers keep using fear and violence to get what they want, the police now have more, and better, ways to stop robberies. With the latest technology, **CCTV** cameras are making a real difference. They not only **deter** robbers, they also help to catch them. The latest **forensic** science is now better at tracing criminals than ever before. That is why robbers often cop it in the end!

Caught on camera

We are being watched. In most towns and cities we are filmed in streets and shops. Every day CCTV cameras record robbers at work.

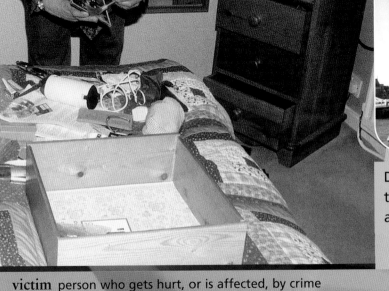

Do you ever notice the cameras that are watching you?

victim person who gets hurt, or is affected, by crime
witness someone who sees a crime happen

Find out more

Answer to quiz on page 24

If you want to find out more about the criminal underworld, why not have a look at these books:

Behind the Scenes: Solving a Crime,
   Peter Mellet (Heinemann Library, 1999)
Forensic Files: Investigating Murders,
   Paul Dowswell (Heinemann Library, 2004)
Forensic Files: Investigating Thefts and Heists,
   Alex Woolf (Heinemann Library, 2004)
Just the Facts: Cyber Crime,
   Neil McIntosh (Heinemann Library, 2002)

Answer to quiz on page 24

No one is truly certain of the real answer! But it is more likely to be c). By the mid 1800s, a British policeman was called a "copper" because he "copped" or caught criminals.

Young thief

In 2002 in San Bernardino, California, USA, a 14-year-old girl was charged with robbing 2 banks. She was believed to be the youngest person accused of bank robbery in San Bernardino. Not surprising!

Did you know?

This table shows the number of robberies in different countries around the world in 2000.

Country	Number of robberies
Spain	497,262
USA	409,670*
Mexico	215,120
South Africa	197,038
Russia	132,393
Chile	110,672
UK	95,154
Indonesia	61,260
Germany	59,414
Poland	53,533
Italy	37,726
Venezuela	34,975
India	28,411*
Canada	27,012
Colombia	24,537
France	24,304
Australia	23,314
Ukraine	21,429
Costa Rica	19,241*
The Netherlands	18,630

* Figures are for 1999.

So they say...

Every day an average of twenty banks are robbed somewhere in the world. The average amount taken is around £1600!

Glossary

abandon leave something behind

attempted robbery trying to commit robbery, but caught in the act

bond certificate promising payment of money

CCTV close circuit television

census counting of people in a country, city, or town

chaos great confusion, when lots of things are happening

civil war war between people of one country

deter put someone off doing something

disqualified banned from doing something

fake copy made to look like the real thing

far-fetched hard to believe or imagine

fiction not real – stories that are made-up

Flying Squad police unit investigating bank robbery, jewel thefts, and armed robberies

forensic scientific investigation to help solve crimes

gangster member of a gang of criminals

heist robbery that is carefully planned and organized

highwayman person who robs travellers on a highway

homicide killing, or murder, of one person by another

insure promise by a company to pay money to someone if their property is damaged, or stolen

kidnap carry off a person by force, or against his or her will

life sentence being sent to prison for the rest of a person's life

marshal US government officer similar to a sheriff

matron woman who worked in a police station or prison with women prisoners

mugging robbing in the street with threats or violence

organized crime large, organized groups of criminals

Picasso famous 20th-century painter

priceless too valuable to have a price

recovered get something back again after it has been stolen

sapphire blue precious stone

stagecoach wagon pulled by horses, carrying mail or passengers

suspect someone thought to have committed a crime

truncheon short, thick stick carried by police officers as a weapon

vault locked room for keeping valuables in at a bank

victim person who gets hurt, or is affected by, crime

witness someone who sees a crime happen

airport robberies
  18–19
art robbers 16–17, 40
Australia 25, 27,
  42, 45

bank robbers 5, 7, 8–9,
  14, 15, 30, 31, 32,
  33, 39, 40, 44, 45
Belgium 12
bonds 13
Bonnie and Clyde 4, 33
Bow Street Runners
  24, 25
Brazil 41
Brinks Mat robbery
  20–21
bungled robberies 11,
  38–41
burglars 5
car chases 29
CCTV cameras 40, 43
child robbers 41, 44
"cops" 24
credit card theft 8
crime statistics 4, 9,
  28, 42, 45

diamonds 12, 22, 23
dogs 26–27

Egypt 6

films and television
  programmes 4, 10,
  18, 24, 34–37

Flying Squad 23, 28
forensic science 42, 43

gangsters 7
Germany 30, 39, 45
getaway cars 30,
  31, 33
gold bars 20, 21

heists 18–23, 33
highwaymen 7

India 41, 45
Ireland 31

jewel robbers 12, 15,
  18, 22–23

LAPD 28–29, 35
Lebanon 15

Malaysia 38
marshals 25, 28
Millennium robbery
  22–23
mugging 4, 5, 13, 42

Netherlands 17, 45
Norway 17
Noye, Kenneth 21

oldest robber in the
  world 14
organized crime 19

pickpockets 5
pirates 7

river police 41
Robin Hood 32
Romania 32

shoplifters 5, 39
Spain 4, 45
stagecoach robbers 7

tomb robbers 6
train robbers 10–11
truncheons 25

United Kingdom (UK)
  6, 11, 13, 15, 16,
  20–23, 24–25, 26,
  33, 35, 39, 42, 45
United States (US) 7,
  8–11, 14, 16, 18–19,
  25, 26, 27, 28–29,
  30, 31–33, 34, 35,
  38, 40, 42, 44, 45

Vikings 7

"wanted posters" 35
watchmen 6, 24
women police officers
  28, 29
women robbers 31,
  33, 40

Titles in the *True Crime* series include:

Hardback: 1844 438120

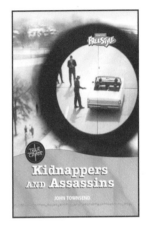

Hardback: 1844 438112

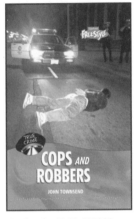

Hardback: 1844 438139

Hardback: 1844 438104

Hardback: 1844 438090

Find out about other Freestyle titles on our website www.raintreepublishers.co.uk